Thoughts
for all
Occasions

Original
Epigrams

by

MICHAEL LIPSEY

BRISTOL
PARK
BOOKS
NEW YORK

Originally published in two Volumes as *I Thought So* and *I Thought So Volume 2*

First BRISTOL PARK BOOKS edition published in 2014

BRISTOL PARK BOOKS
252 WEST 38TH STREET
NEW YORK, NY 10018

BRISTOL PARK BOOKS is a registered trademark of BRISTOL PARK BOOKS, INC.

Published by arrangement with Cypress House

Library of Congress Control Number: 2013951758

ISBN: 978-0-88486-543-8

E-Book ISBN: 978-0-88486-545-2

Cover and Text Design by Keira McGuinness.

Printed in the United States of America

Contents

About Epigrams

An epigram is a few words equaling many, a distilled thought. Webster's Dictionary defines an epigram as "A concise clever, often paradoxical statement" i.e. short pieces of wisdom often witty or satiric. It can convey a large idea and also make you think or smile. The original epigrams in this book are arranged by Art & Literature and Attitude to Wealth and Work. They cover a whole range of categories including Food, Friendship, Health, Life, Love, Manners, Marriage, Politics, Religion and many others. These sayings are quick ways of telling a long story in a few words; a snapshot instead of a panorama, a miniature, not a mural. They get right to the point because it is the moral of the tale, the hard lesson learned that enable you to observe, discuss and ponder life's large questions.

—Michael Lipsey

Art & Literature

Western acting is as stylized
as the Noh theater of Japan—
we're just used to the conventions.

~

Things turn our well in light opera
and badly in heavy opera.

~

You can't write about things that can't be
put into words—but poets never stop trying.

~

Spam writers are the first authors
to use the entire keyboard.

~

Art worth consuming ripens
in about a hundred years.

Originality is the sauce that makes
familiar things interesting.

~

No one loves words more than a two-year-old
who is just learning what they mean.

~

Good to have a large vocabulary,
but even better to use it sparingly.

~

Acclaim may be gratifying to an artist,
but it cuts into studio time.

~

The movies get longer and the popcorn gets bigger,
and there is about as much substance
in each of them.

~

Rock is a concert at which it is impossible to sleep.

Some commas are just a place to rest for a spell,
on your trek through the sentence.

~

Writer's block can generally be cured by writing.

~

An angry poet can write nothing but doggerel.

~

Write in your true voice, and you will be heard.

~

When you discover the thing that really interests
you, other interests begin to drop away.

~

The voices of my angels offer encouragement but
my demons drive me to do my best work.

~

To write well you must be a ruthless editor.

Keep a copy of this book in your pocket in case
you should have to make an impromptu speech,
or be stuck in an elevator for six hours.

∾

By reading the classics we learn that
everything has already been said.

∾

The raw material of art is life, just as wine
is made from sun, dirt, and water.

∾

Your first creative act, on the wall
with a crayon, was greeted with horror.

∾

You could fill the Hollywood Bowl
with forgotten stars.

∾

A writer must write, and write and write.

When the fine arts become as creative
as advertising, we will be living
in another Renaissance.

≈

The collector gets more pleasure
from the painting than the artist does,
because the artist sees only an attempt.

≈

The problem with fiction is that it is just that.

≈

The most valuable thing in my wallet
is my library card.

≈

You are always at home in an art museum,
because art is a universal language.

≈

An autobiography is just an authorized biography.

On matters of taste, everyone is always right.

∾

Computers increase writing
while decreasing literacy.

∾

Call me a serious music listener and I will smile.

∾

There are patterns and rhythms everywhere
if you can see them and hear them.

∾

I've seen plays that are longer than my life.

∾

I believe in any religion that has celestial music.

∾

Hollywood has sunk to the point where
Oscars are awarded for mumbling.

Everyone knew music until
recording was invented.

≈

There should be no such thing as a concert hall
without a dance floor.

≈

There is music that makes you dance,
even if you don't.

≈

Fiction is gossip about imaginary friends.

≈

At the symphony half close their eyes
to concentrate on the music
and the other half to sleep.

≈

You will find few murder mystery readers in the
neighborhoods where people are often murdered.

Writers should give thanks that a Shakespeare
only comes along once in 400 years.

∾

A poem can only be translated
by writing another poem.

∾

Fiction writing is an attempt
to make a story go somewhere.

∾

Money follows culture,
because culture validates money.

∾

A playwright often runs out of ideas
in the middle of the second act.

∾

There is nothing more conducive to falling asleep
than propping myself up in bed with a book
I have been looking forward to reading.

To be a good writer,
allow very few adverbs into your life.

∾

We must grant young artists the courtesy of
pretending to be outraged by their spirited
attempts, but the truth is that nothing
outrages us anymore.

∾

A poem should be more like a painting
than like a novel.

∾

There are writers who have
exactly one perfect book in them.

ℰ

Attitude

*H*aving a passion for anything
is reason enough to live.

~

You wouldn't like to think of yourself
as a discouraging person—
so be an encouraging person!

~

Those who need drama in their lives
generally get poor reviews.

~

Every day you have only twenty-four hours to live.

~

From low self-esteem comes an
insatiable craving for praise.

Was it a dull party, or was I the dull party?

∽

Bad to have all kinds of excuses—
far worse if you believe them.

∽

When we slip into bitterness we
lose sight of the sweetness of life.

∽

It only takes one small piece of
good news to make my day.

∽

Mind your own business very well.

∽

I had a problem with authority when I was young,
and fifty years later I still have one, but it
has become more discriminating.

The carefree brain has room for
thinking interesting thoughts,
but the worried brain is at capacity.

～

Like a worn-out rubber stamp,
some people make almost no impression.

～

Real ability is knowing something
to do in almost any situation.

～

Unhappiness has always had its devotees.

～

I would like to have a button on the dashboard
of my car labeled LAUNCH MISSILE.

～

Manipulation fails when you see it as such.

Tourists complain endlessly,
but real travelers suffer cheerfully.

∾

The neurotic who divides his time
between regretting the past and worrying
about the future has no presence at all.

∾

You can only help the willing—the obstinate ones
will create difficulties that will exhaust you.

∾

The magic ingredient of persuasion is a talent for
seeing things from the other person's point of view.

∾

The different drummer I march
to beats in my heart.

∾

On a day like this I feel like I could…but every
day is a day like this!

If you really believe that all men are created equal,
you are comfortable in any company.

~

You can be funny with people who have no sense
of humor—and you can also get
your head bitten off.

~

If you let resentment take root,
it will spring up all over your mind.

~

You can make someone happy,
but you can't make someone be happy.

~

When you toss a cat in the air it always lands on
its feet—there are people like that.

~

The reason the water is so cold is that you are only
in it up to your knees.

Be a warm person.

~

To an awakened mind the best place is here and
the best time is now.

~

Welcome yourself to the day with a smile in the
bathroom mirror.

~

Always carry yourself as if your fans are watching.

~

Be kind to yourself.

~

The best advice ever given is "Let it go."

~

Where others see complexity, the person of
action sees the thing that needs to be done.

Pay attention to what needs to be done—
not to what should have been done.

∽

If you are doing your best there is plenty to do.

∽

Always get up on the right side of bed.

∽

Your life has a Start Menu, just like Windows.

∽

Self-compassion, but never self-pity.

∽

Let my spirit rise above this sea of negativity.

∽

A pessimist believes that everything is
for the worse—and there is nothing
worse than being a pessimist.

A fearful person lives on Planet Scary.

∾

If your eyes are open there is plenty to see.

∾

Your thirst can never be satisfied
if your glass is always half empty.

∾

You can always give yourself one more chance.

∾

Just tell your neurotic inner voice to shut up.

∾

A light heart is young until the day it stops.

∾

There are times when I am in serious
danger of taking myself seriously.

Be useful, keeping in mind that
complaining is not useful.

≈

Every day of my life—
this incredible adventure!

≈

Never say bad things about anyone
and you will be adored.

≈

See everything for the first time

≈

If you fail to understand failure—you can
walk through fire.

≈

I'm having a bad day" is a self-fulfilling prophecy.

On the morning of the last day of Pompeii the people had many important things on their minds.

~

Sing the blues, if you must, but don't live them.

~

The pains in your legs are a pleasure, when you're nearing the top.

~

The biggest head start is a good attitude.

~

Don't waste good news on a pessimist.

~

Could you give me a hand? I'm moving the world.

~

Always keep your charm turned on.

~

Business

The marketplace may be efficient, but
no one has ever said that it is kind.

~

Try to get customer service and
you will see that we live in Babel.

~

The ego rapidly expands to fill the larger office.

~

A sinking economy causes fear and
fear sinks the economy.

~

It is hard to maintain equanimity
when you have just lost a lot of money.

A dull business meeting gets a lot more interesting
when you realize that your job is on the line.

~

The theory that customers will put up
with anything is called "voicemail."

~

Watching a televangelist at work
confirms my faith in the free market.

~

Expert opinions are bought and
sold like any other commodity.

~

To play the game you must either
know the rules or make the rules.

~

That banks are eager to lend you money
should be warning enough.

Being self-employed is a modern way
of saying that you live by your wits.

≈

A thing is obviously worth what it sells for—
but this is only true at the moment of the transaction.

≈

How many who curse spam
have ever tasted Spam?

≈

A sales force is motivated by greed
and driven by fear.

≈

All advertising is spam.

≈

The enormous advertising industry is
an inverted pyramid resting on the
shaky premise that advertising works.

To survive in a corporate office you must
either be doing something useful, or appear
to be doing something useful.

~

The favor bank is always open for new deposits.

~

You can tell when you are nearing the center of
power, because the suits are better fitting.

~

Ten seconds of thought could have
prevented a year of damage control.

~

As the general can lose a battle but not his
command, so the executive can make a
decision that costs thousands of people
their jobs and not lose his own.

Capitalism is always thinking of ways
to eliminate the small operator.

❧

The business traveler pretends to work, as if to
deny that so much of his life is being wasted.

❧

If your word is your bond, it is reasonable
for it to carry a very high interest rate.

❧

There would be no stock market if the bulls
weren't right a little more often than the bears.

❧

The stock market smiles on a company that
dumps thousands of well-paid older workers,
most of whom will never again have decent
jobs—because the market has no heart.

One of the triumphs of capitalism
was turning "shop" into a verb.

≈

Companies take booths at trade shows
to prove that they exist.

≈

Ambition is always naked,
because there is no way to clothe it.

≈

An Indian casino is where the white man
goes to get scalped.

≈

There is nothing less entertaining
than business entertainment.

≈

It's the sure things that turn out really badly.

The answer to almost any
legal question is expensive.

~

When Asia discovers individuality,
they will bury us.

~

The only subject that endlessly
fascinates the media is the media.

~

They can make the employees say, "Thank you sir,
have a nice day." But they can't make them add
inflection, emphasis, or eye contact.

~

The only kind of snake you can trust
is the kind that crawls on the ground.

~

Culture

It's easy to stay current—all you have to do
is read twenty-four hours a day.

~

California is always also a state of mind.

~

To a farmer, a close neighbor is a mile away;
to a city apartment dweller, a neighbor snoring
on the other side of the bedroom wall.

~

Entering a new culture is like having to fit
a second skin on top of your old one.

~

There is someone interesting living on any
block of any street anywhere in the world.

Young people will travel halfway around the world
to sit in a bar with other young tourists.

～

We Americans are mongrels, always eager to start
yapping about the ethnicity of our ancestors.

～

The mind of an intellectual is poisoned
by even a tinge of bigotry.

～

Americans do not save because in our culture
we gain more status from consumption.

～

When traveling we are refreshed
by the differentness of things.

～

The observer of society must always
be standing a little apart.

We have no problem with illegal immigrants
ministering to many of our needs—
the problem is having to minister
to some of theirs.

≈

There are a thousand different
"real Americas—each as real as the next.

≈

When people of two very different
cultures meet, they often share a feeling
that the other is very backward.

≈

Thanks to the grinding poverty of the natives,
our vacation was a terrific bargain!

≈

An American conversation: 'I'm Polish."
"So when did you come here?" "Well, actually
my grandparents came here in 1920."

This work of civilization has barely begun.

~

You can hear worse language on a golf course
than at a boxing march.

~

There are countries where we are loved
and countries where we are hated—
but trying to resist the onslaught of American
culture would be like trying to repel the weather.

~

White comes in pink to tan,
and black comes in tan to ebony.

~

A culture has as much will to live as a species has.

~

The white person who gets nicely tanned
on a Third-World beach would still
not care to be mistaken for a native.

There are people who have a gift for
looking distinguished, and nothing more.

～

We carry our ethnic heritage
like an invisible costume.

～

We attach more importance to skin color
than to hair or eye color because we are racists.

～

America is divided between those
who love lawns and those who love grass.

～

Working class is when you take better care
of your car than of your body.

～

There is nothing the city offers
that is compensation for never
seeing a sky filled with stars.

Cultures are most interesting where they intersect.

The Midwest is flat and the people there
are more levelheaded.

Half of what we brought from Europe
deserved to be left behind as fast as possible.

We ask people about their ethnic origins
and then we foolishly think that
we know something about them.

We love and cherish the immigrants we know,
and hate and fear the ones we don't know.

The weaker the culture,
the more it fears intermarriage.

Death

*T*here is no ego too large
to fit into a standard grave.

~

Achieving a posthumous reputation
proves that death is no glass ceiling.

~

Many small things annoy you—
take comfort in how much less annoying
they will be when you are dead.

~

What is your hurry?
You know where your journey ends.

~

You can't call a dead person and
tell her how much you love her.

I only ask you to remember me dancing.

≈

When I die I would like people to say,
"He was a good listener."

≈

If you plan to confess some great secret
on your deathbed, do it a little before
you lose the ability to speak.

≈

Death is the hardest truth;
all the others are bearable.

≈

The man who is acting most naturally
is at his own funeral.

≈

I don't have a minute to spare—
life is calling me, and I have death on hold.

At least let me put my photos
in the album before I croak.

~

The hardest universe to imagine is
one in which we do not exist.

~

A great pleasure is the cessation of pain.

~

If you are comfortable with death you have
one less major problem to deal with in life.

~

When I'm dead I won't care what people say
about me—so why should I wait to
not care until I'm dead?

~

The widower is more likely to
be merry than the widow.

This old cloak that I call my skin is mottled
and worn, but I think it will last me.

∼

Dropping dead is a much more convenient
way to go than the illness method.

∼

No one can identify the old photo of
the man with the beard, so we toss it, and
that is his last appearance in the world.

∼

Did you ever arrive somewhere, your mind full of
thoughts, and realize with a start that your
body has been driving for the past hour?

∼

Let your life story have a happy ending.

∼

I wouldn't like to be cremated to
end up in a shoebox in the closet

The older you get
the more interesting your skin becomes.

~

In a few years you'll be dust, and you're in
a rage because someone cut in front of you?

~

Where violence is part of everyday life
it is no deterrence to violence.

~

If you have a disease that is absolutely fatal,
and you rely on quack medicine,
you are none the worse for it.

~

Don't try to cheer up someone
who is properly mourning.

~

Yes, there are some kindly journalists—
they write the obituaries.

When I'm feeling discouraged and I comfort
myself by thinking this too shall pass,
a little voice is saying, "One day it won't."

~

Longevity is no blessing if you've
always been miserable.

~

Suicide is the last word on the subject.

~

Write something about yourself on your photos
so your descendants will know who you were.

~

There is one piece of bad news that
you don't have to worry about hearing,
because it will be about you.

My only protection is in this constant worry.

A consolation of becoming very elderly is knowing that your passing will not cause so much pain.

What would you like to be remembered for?

Food

A good cook is adventurous—
great cook is insane.

≈

Try to weigh yourself on a day
when gravity is not too high.

≈

The body arrives in front of the refrigerator
and the door opens by some mysterious means.

≈

Food is delicious in inverse proportion
to its health benefits.

≈

You can't talk seriously about food
with a skinny person.

The good news is that I love to cook—
the bad news is that I look it.

∾

Prove that eating broccoli extended my life
by a year and I might do it, but if it was
only a month, it wouldn't be worth it.

∾

"Fast food"—the very words give me indigestion.

∾

Does the world exist before
I have my first cup of coffee?

∾

Dinner should be a leisurely journey to dessert.

∾

There are more people in the world
who eat insects than who eat truffles.

Don't expect to find a great lover in
someone who is not interested in food.

∾

There isn't always sex,
but there is always chocolate.

Vegetarians occupy the high moral ground,
but my stomach is not a moralist.

∾

An oyster is the only thing that a
civilized person swallows alive.

∾

A vegetarian and a cannibal can agree
that no animals should be harmed
in making their dinners.

∾

We didn't get to the top of the
food chain by eating broccoli.

The pleasure of eating something awful,
like a snail, is in the sauce.

❧

I will die happy if I outlive some of the people
who keep telling me that my diet is unhealthy.

❧

The ordering of an 800-calorie dessert must be
preceded by the incantation "I really shouldn't…."

❧

If the pig knew why it was being fattened
it would lose its appetite.

❧

Open your best bottle and cook the chicken in the
wine that you were planning to drink it with.

❧

I can't control my weight because
I'm constantly being attacked by food.

It is dangerous to be alone
in a room with a large pizza.

≈

There are those who go to the store and select
each cherry, and those who just grab them by the
handful—I'd like to have my cherries selected
by the former, but eat them with the latter.

≈

Food is love, but love is not sugar-free and fat-free.

≈

The adventure of eating cherries is that
each one is a little different from the last.

≈

Chicken is spoken in the kitchens of all nations.

≈

It must be strange for a Chinese immigrant to
hear someone saying, "So, you want Chinese?"

In WASP heaven, the food is
nothing to write home about.

❧

Grabbing a check can be generosity,
or it can be an act of aggression.

❧

Eat and drink lightly when you need to think—
satiation is the enemy of contemplation.

❧

Any wine worth drinking
goes well with chocolate.

❧

When you are a good cook you are frequently
cursed as follows: "You should open a restaurant."

❧

If you want to live a long and healthy life,
keep yourself a little hungry.

The pot calls the kettle black, and the teakettle
calls the pot dull-witted, and the saucepan
calls the teakettle shrill, and the skillet
calls the saucepan rude, and the casserole calls
the skillet hot-tempered, and the kettle calls
the casserole stodgy.

~

Resist the urge to babble when there is a
lull in the dinner-party conversation.

~

Antacids make the eating of many
wonderful things possible.

~

I love to cook for people who bring good wine
and good conversation—and wash dishes.

~

You will tire of eating lobster before
you will tire of eating French fries.

While we discuss the fine points of poaching
a salmon, elsewhere in the world someone is
cooking a rat on a stick over some burning trash.

~

The abundance of food we celebrate
on Thanksgiving is our blessing—
and the overabundance is our curse.

~

Tampering with the recipe for an ethnic dish
that has been perfected over hundreds of years
is like singing a beautiful folk song…off-key.

~

The secret ingredient is usually ketchup.

~

I am always amazed at what I just ate.

~

Friendship

I generally get along pretty well with
myself but I have my moments.

❧

The enemy of my enemy might be my friend,
but not a friend I would like to
have over for the weekend.

❧

The meanest man in the world still loves his dog.

❧

With the gift of being able to see things
through the eyes of others come the
gifts of sympathy and understanding.

❧

The deeper you go into the thing
that interests you, the smaller the circle
with whom you can discuss it.

A grudge-master has the art of
cultivating a slight into a major insult.

∾

Eventually you learn to make
no firm plans with the flaky.

∾

A good reason to make new friends is
that your old ones have heard all your stories.

∾

When your best friends are books they
will always be there for you.

∾

If getting together with a friend requires
comparing your schedules for the next two
months, your lives are out of control.

∾

A man tells the joke but forgets the punch line,
a woman tells the punch line but forgets the joke.

Always keep an open space
in your life for a new friend.

～

When you are young, you talk all night with your
friends about nothing—and it seems profound.

～

When you say, "My mind is like that,"
do you mean that you are only
capable of certain thoughts?

～

You can sense hostility, even when
it is under lock and key.

～

It's surprising how much of a relief
it can be to give up on someone.

～

Insulting a friend is like pouring
a herbicide on your garden.

Our society is only the world of people
who include us in their plans.

～

A funny story about yourself might
be a mean story if it's about a friend.

～

The shallower your notion of friendship,
the more people you can count as friends.

～

Choose wisely the people you invite into your
life—and the people you invite out of your life.

～

Forget anything your friends
would rather you forgot.

～

We value people we have known for a long
time—because they prove we have a past.

When people talk about total loyalty,
they are talking about a dog.

∾

We sometimes find ourselves in a place where
everyone looks like someone we know,
but no one is.

∾

We are in danger of forgetting our friends
when our lives are going exceptionally well.

∾

We call our numerous acquaintances friends,
but one is blessed to have even a few true friends.

∾

Duration inflates the value of friendships.

∾

Many generous people would die before
they would ask a friend for help.

We know enough not to rub a cat
the wrong way, but not a person.

∼

You get more mileage from
alcohol in good company.

∼

If you have youthful friends who are dissatisfied
and unhappy, expect to endure their bitterness
and grudges as they grow older.

∼

When we say someone is a "real character"
we are not talking about character.

∼

We often ask for advice when
the last thing we want is advice.

∼

How could anyone not like me,
when I'm so charming?

Make friends with people who enlarge your world.

～

An interesting conversation is like two
people holding an object and turning it in their
hands to view all sides.

～

When we visit very old friends we are
young together for a few hours.

～

Try hard to be amusing and you will certainly fail.

～

A real conversation, which is something rare,
is a series of linked statements.

～

You can be most alone in the busiest places.

℃

Health

*I*f I walked to the gym I wouldn't
need it so much.

❦

Alcohol is a preservative, but not for brains.

❦

Nervous people make me nervous.

❦

If you want to hear something profound,
don't ask a wino.

❦

People who love people drive carefully.

❦

Football is hard bodies colliding on the screen
and soft ones sinking into the sofa.

Middle age is when you grow your middle.

❧

Your body is a temple given to you by God—
defile it and you will receive Biblical punishments.

❧

A psychologist will interpret a dream
of looking for a bathroom without
asking if you woke up having to pee.

❧

Crazy people are only a little crazier.

❧

You think you've been handling a difficult
situation in your life very well, but then,
suddenly, you are overwhelmed by stress.

❧

Surviving a serious illness puts
everything on the table.

When we are children the world can be a scary
place, but as we grow older it is our body
that is the scary place.

～

One of the benefits of growing older is
that you get a lot of extra skin.

～

The meat industry puts hormones in our beef and
the drug industry puts hormones in our women.

～

When you're on a diet,
food will leap into your mouth.

～

Weight is a boomerang; it just keeps coming back.

～

The most carcinogenic substance
you are exposed to is sunlight.

You get fat in the moments between when you
know you should stop and when you do.

~

I only allow myself dessert on special
occasions—and what occasion is not special?

~

Eventually a hypochondriac dies,
to everyone's amazement.

~

Does the proverb "Physician, heal thyself
apply to psychologists"?

~

Don't eat anything with a lot of
small print on the package.

~

God, moving in his mysterious ways,
seems to be fattening us.

What makes us crazy differs from person to person-but there is always something that does.

❧

One of the medical skills is stating the diagnosis with conviction.

❧

Drive as if all the other drivers on the road are drunk.

❧

You can't argue with an obsession but you can humor it.

❧

Just because you're an adult doesn't mean you don't need to have a bedtime.

❧

Hypochondria and quack medicine are joined at the hip.

Everyone should be allowed one phobia
without being considered a nut case.

～

The driven will drive six hours
each way to relax for a weekend.

～

Shaking hands is an efficient method we
have developed for exchanging our microbes.

～

I'm happy with my weight—on the moon.

～

You can't know anyone else's mind
if you don't even know your own.

～

When we can't find our car, we worry that it has
been stolen-and when we do find it, we worry
that we are losing our minds.

My obsessions are my "interests"—
your obsessions are your craziness.

❧

The doctor gives comfort by sending you home
with a meaningless name for your symptoms.

❧

No, you haven't lost your mind—
it's rattling around in there somewhere.

❧

Having a personal trainer is like being a dog.

❧

At some point in the evening
you realize that you are asleep.

❧

Our thoughts are a tangled mixture of
reality and unreality—and this stew makes
life interesting and existence bearable.

It is not human nature not to worry.

~

Skinny people look terrific — with their clothes on.

~

Your therapist should know you better
than you know your therapist.

~

There is no such a thing as a strong back.

~

When you have hay fever the universe
is composed of pollen.

~

Addictions crowd out other interests.

~

If the universe were fair, good-hearted people
would never get heart attacks.

Progression is the opposite of progress,
when you're talking about a disease.

∼

How did Gluttony become
more popular than Lust?

∼

When getting an opinion from a surgeon, keep in
mind that surgeons make their living by cutting.

∼

The office guys in the gym now have bigger
muscles than the factory guys in the bar.

∼

The benefit of a major health scare is that
it diminishes all your other little worries.

∼

Exercise may not make us thinner, live longer, or
prevent cancer—but it does make us feel virtuous.

A cocktail is a very pretty drug.

Dark chocolate or martinis, antidepressants or
ginseng, coffee or chardonnay, aerobics,
television, crosswords or crack cocaine,
we all must have our drugs.

My country 'tis obese.

Your mother taught you how to eat,
but she didn't teach you how to stop.

Let yourself be inebriated by nothing, except life.

Popular medical advice contradicts itself daily.

Home

*B*efore you can get something done you
have to know where that thing is.

≈

The war against clutter is like the war
against terror—it must be unrelenting.

≈

Clutter is the material expression
of mental disorder.

≈

It takes a hundred years for a
new neighborhood to become charming.

≈

We live out our lives in just a few
well-worn spots in our homes.

Pack rats generally don't miss the
small things you throw away when they
aren't around, as long as you don't go overboard.

≈

Growing up in a place that everyone leaves,
your mental bags are always packed.

≈

The longest job a contractor can get
is remodeling his own home.

≈

Nature abhors a lawn.

≈

A bargain on something you didn't
really need is no bargain at all.

≈

When home is a happy place,
one is happy to be at home.

There is plenty to do at home, without going out
and causing more problems in the world.

~

We invite a stranger to make himsdf comfortable
in the living room we never set foot in.

~

One day something in the garage
will prove to be useful.

~

It is impossible to paint a room the
exact color you had in mind.

~

Real hospitality is being invited
to eat in the kitchen, like family.

~

My home is always as neat as a pin—
five minutes before the company arrives.

Most Americans couldn't describe the place
where they live because it is a vast,
incomprehensible, suburban sprawl.

~

We may be the preeminent world power,
but I'm not even a regional power at home.

~

Suburban life is boring and pleasant and safe,
and that suits most Americans just fine.

~

To the extent that you think your house
is an investment, it is less of a home,
and more of a commodity that you
ought to unload at peak value.

~

Every tradesman knows that houses can make
otherwise normal people get very crazy.

A bad neighborhood is one
in which the intolerable is tolerated.

～

Teenagers raised in endless subdivisions and
shopping malls laced together by, freeways
understand alienation without knowing the word.

～

When you are deep in thought is not a good time
to be washing the best china.

～

Homeless people have often
thrown away a few homes.

～

There is no such thing as a clean house,
from the point of view of a microbiologist, an
allergist, a health inspector, and environmental
chemist, or your mother.

An old house is moody in bad weather,
creaking and sighing.

≈

What am I doing this weekend?
Must I always be doing?

≈

"Your house is thinking,
"These people too shall pass."

≈

A walk around a suburban subdivision
with cul-de-sacs is a walk to nowhere.

≈

At a certain age we say, "I will live out
my days in this place."

≈

The true gardener can no more relax in her garden
than a farmer would relax in his field of corn.

℃

Life

*T*here are three halves to anything
that is done by halves.

~

Each day brings a new problem, and a previous
day's crisis solves itself without your intervention.

~

Life is a challenge — if you enjoy picking fights.

~

A few words can contain the design for a life.

~

Don't offer philosophy when hearing of tragedy.

~

A successful person feels a little less
a failure than the rest of us.

Trying to be "philosophical" about a
disaster in your life is small consolation.

∼

Looking back on my life, I wonder if there
is someone who shares a regret with me.

∼

Other people can make us sad, but only we
can make ourselves truly miserable.

∼

With prosperity and leisure comes the luxury
of being able to make problems for ourselves.

∼

If you have made more good decisions than bad
ones, you have had a better-than-average life.

∼

We often know the answer to one of life's
questions, but we are afraid to ask the question.

Having a major setback in life
tells you what you are made of.

❧

We change long before we realize
that we have changed.

❧

If you must be a loser in life, try to be a good loser.

❧

We divide our time between the universe that
exists and another that exists only
in our imagination.

❧

There is no brotherhood of all mankind,
but there might be a sisterhood.

❧

You have as much work to do
on your life as in your work.

There is just enough time in the moment before
we ski into the tree to regret our indecisiveness.

～

First we play, then we work, then we play again.

～

In the time it takes to read this a
multitude of lives have begun and ended.

～

If you are completely organized, you
probably don't have time for much else.

～

It is in a rare moment of complete clarity
that one makes a major life decision.

～

Birthdays are milestones in
what we have not accomplished.

One becomes an adult by an
abrupt series of discoveries.

~

A new interest can become a new life.

~

The purposeful life must struggle with the
constant maddening distractions of everyday life.

~

Stupid isn't making a bad mistake in life—
we all do—it's repeating that bad mistake.

~

Difficult passages in life are rougher
for those used to smooth sailing.

~

Don't try to seem like anything to anybody—
just be your best self.

Those who prefer to make bad decisions
have little use for good advice.

≈

How to live is a more difficult problem
than the origin of the universe.

≈

Whether you're asking for a job, a date, a favor,
or a loan, desperation is the kiss of death.

≈

We are the fishermen who weave the
nets that ensnare us.

≈

I didn't turn out like they expected—
but neither did I turn out like I expected.

≈

Many pass their lives simply
waiting for them to be over.

Don't let yourself be rushed
into anything by anybody.

~

Every time I lost my way I discovered a new path.

~

Don't bother waiting for it all to happen—
it only happens if you make it happen.

~

A complicated life is more of a problem for
family and friends than for the person
who causes all the complications.

~

You can't live a life that is
both driven and reflective.

~

For best results examine your life
frequently and adjust as necessary.

It's not surprising how much goes wrong,
but how much goes right.

~

The average human situation is that things could
be a lot better, but they could also be a lot worse.

~

The main problem in philosophy is how to live—
and that is why philosophy is the only field of
study that does not progress.

~

The predictable thing about life is that it will be
difficult—the unpredictable thing is how.

~

Freedom is the ability to decide
what you are going to do today.

~

It is always easy to make your life difficult.

We who live in the slow lane like
seeing empty pages in our calendars.

≈

I may be a product of my circumstances, but
I refuse to live my life under such limitations.

≈

The road not taken was not your path.

≈

When you accept that you control nothing
in the world except your own behavior,
life becomes much less complicated.

≈

Don't fuss.

≈

The more important a person might be
in your life, the more things you
tend to notice about them.

I would like to live in a well-designed life.

A happy life can be the result of a
determination to be happy and to
ignore the usual neurotic thoughts.

Don't let your life story be all fish that got away.

$\mathcal{L}ove$

$\mathcal{A}$ love affair becomes a relationship when someone says "We…."

~

I'll be your world, if you'll be my mine.

~

Never forget that you are married to a very beautiful woman.

~

True love does not need a lot of space.

~

If you sleep with people who have troubles, you will certainly catch them.

~

Lovers are a world.

We can exist without love,
but we can't live without it.

∾

Falling in love is the second best thing in life;
knowing that it will always last is the best.

∾

Whichever sex you are, the mystery of the
opposite one keeps life interesting.

∾

Don't waste your time trying
to warm up a cold fish.

∾

There is a hundred times more sex
in the world than lovemaking.

∾

A cult leader creates a community with his
charisma and destroys it with his libido.

Some men are only capable of
real intercourse after lovemaking.

~

Was I really in love with that snake?

~

The moon is more flattering than
any lighting arranged by experts.

~

You can't buy love, but people
spend a lot of money trying.

~

How can our relationship grow when
you don't respect my need to discuss
everything that is wrong with you?

~

Love begins with attraction, which is
the great mystery of our physiology.

The people browsing the relationship section
of a bookstore may not be very good at
relationships—but they're working on it.

∾

It is possible to be in love with someone
you really don't like all that much.

∾

Sex is slowly parting ways with reproduction.

∾

Money is sexy—but the less sexy you are,
the more money it takes to make you so.

∾

A first date is not grounds for an interrogation.

∾

After spending years finding the perfect mate
we find that we are incapable of perfect mating.

Online dating would work better
if a method were discovered for
piping pheromones over the Internet.

∾

The sexual athlete begins his game
by serving an absolutely great opening line.

∾

An unhappy couple fools no one.

∾

If your heart is big enough the world
can fit inside of it.

∾

Sleeping alone is not even good for sleeping.

∾

Our first reaction to being jilted is
that it must be some kind of mistake.

If your parents really loved you, you always feel
you are a worthwhile person, no matter
what happens in life.

~

We know what attracts us, but haven't a clue
why we find such a person so attractive.

~

If only we spent as much time caressing
each other as we do our keyboards.

~

First there is the silent question:
"If I ask you for a date will you say yes?"

~

Freedom—the enemy of commitment.

~

If you turn into the Spanish Inquisition
on the first date, you probably won't get a second.

The man who is very good at romance
is often not very good at relationships.

≈

Sexiness is a declining asset that still produces a
high rate of interest until it is fully depreciated.

≈

The only treasures we really
have to give are love and kindness.

≈

A singles event is a roomful of
people who haven't lost all hope.

≈

Girls know instinctively how to flirt—
but boys must be taught how to be romantic.

≈

A morning person and a night person—
it will never work.

A single kiss can change your life.

~

Memory has a special place for first times.

~

Sexy, sex, ex—it was a brief affair.

~

Many a bad argument could
have been averted with a hug.

~

First loves are full of misunderstandings.

~

We should have fifty words for
the different kinds of love.

You don't get what you need by being needy.

~

To study first-date behaviors,
go to an art museum.

~

Love is the main event.

~

Let a love affair that is over be over—
remember the good times, but don't look back,
don't replay, don't try to understand, don't look
for lessons, and don't regret anything.

~

When you feel sexy, you are.

Manners

*H*ave sympathy for any personality
defect, except cynicism.

~

Gossip slithers into my ear; may it die there.

~

Don't worry what people think about you,
because they rarely do.

~

It is easy to forgive an insult,
but harder to forget one.

~

We sink financially in order to rise socially.

~

Difficult people are like potholes: there is nothing
to do but go around them.

The cell phone has exhausted all conversational possibilities, and still people are chattering everywhere, about nothing.

≈

Hide your intensity, or it will scare people.

≈

An angry face is never a pretty face.

≈

Some people tend their grudges
as others tend their gardens.

≈

When we socialize we observe, gossip, schmooze,
and keep score, and on the way home we compare
notes with our partner in our researches.

≈

We do not like to believe that
we deserve to be anyone's enemy.

People who always speak their minds
have their fans, but they are few.

≈

Other people are often quite boring,
but we are never boring.

≈

Good character expands your circle of
acquaintance and poor character shrinks it.

≈

Some people are always at a simmer,
ready to boil over.

≈

The wine you serve your guests is of no
consequence compared to the topic you serve.

≈

If you are a fast talker you want to
pick up a slow talker and shake him.

The best method of dealing with
difficult people is the distance method.

❧

We feel slighted when not invited,
even to a very boring social event.

❧

Your travels, your possessions, and your health…
is this the drab inventory of your conversation?

❧

Even a softly spoken insinuation
does not escape our hearing.

❧

One must endure a monologue,
but one does not have to listen to it.

❧

A complainer complains as
naturally as a bird sings.

The last people to arrive are the ones
who always seem to be in a hurry.

~

If people said what was actually on their minds
twice as often, the murder rate would double.

~

Bad table manners ruin more
careers than incompetence.

~

A good listener has no idea
what you are about to say.

~

There is nothing ruder than to be a guest
who is obviously not having a good time.

~

There is no such thing as an impatient listener,
because there is no listening without patience.

The expression "I am really touched" is a
recognition that touch is something
more powerful than words.

~

Ever heard of anyone being
admired for being a gossip?

~

A difficult person does not have an easy life.

~

Don't try to build bridges
with people who burn them.

~

Speech increases in flavor
as you descend in society.

~

You would be less rude to telemarketers if you
considered how unfortunate it is to be one.

The juicier the gossip the more
it diminishes the teller.

～

Why do kindly people usually look that way?

～

Never begin your thanks with
"You shouldn't have…."

～

Angry people are most alive when in a rage.

～

We have an absolute right to mind our own business.

～

To simply be a nice person
is no small achievement.

～

I see a crying infant in the face of the angry man.

It is a rare privilege to encounter greatness—
unless the great one happens to be in a
foul mood, jet-lagged, or half-drunk.

~

Some people would rather lose the
relationship than the argument.

~

The essence of manners is tact,
which few can master.

~

"I always tell it like it is" is the long way
of saying, "I'm a jerk."

~

Remember only your own stupidity.

~

Sarcasm and cynicism are easy,
but irony is mastered by few.

A party to fulfill social obligations
is not a party, it is a ceremony.

~

To appear confident is almost as good
as actually being confident.

~

Don't make a pretense of
modesty by denigrating praise.

~

A proper elevator expression is
friendly but neutral.

~

You never really get to know a taciturn person.

~

There are times when you have to get right in
somebody's face, but it works better
if you keep your voice soft.

A smile is effective at a range of up to thirty feet.

≈

If you could meet your great-great-great grandfather,
you probably would find him very smelly.

≈

If you don't want to raise bigots,
consider what comes out of your mouth.

≈

An apology that is followed with a justification is
no apology at all.

≈

Never tell anyone who is proudly displaying a new
possession that you know where they
could have gotten it for less.

≈

One doesn't just become an old bore,
one must serve one's time as a young bore.

Telling stories is no substitute for
holding up your end of a conversation.

～

There are ways of saying yes
that mean no, and of no that mean yes!

～

Dignity is never in a rush.

～

If a cure were discovered for narcissism,
few would take it.

～

It is tragic, but there are people
who are born without a personality.

～

Must we thank everyone who played
even the most insignificant role in
making this event possible?

A braying laugh betrays humble origins, despite
layers of refinement laid on like frosting.

~

You enjoyed listening to a gossip until
you heard what she said about you.

~

There are two basic personality types: Everything
is a Big Deal and No Big Deal.

~

Easy to say far more than you intended to
when you are being amusing.

~

After you deliver your parting shot you always
think of one that would have been better.

~

I am annoyed that annoying people are
so untroubled by their annoyingness.

We like to gather in public places where
we can be alone with our computers.

~

There is always far more being said
than being heard.

~

Always keep a lash length away
from an irritable person.

~

The three most beautiful words in the
English language are "You were right!"

~

Someone was rude to you?
So let their rudeness be their problem.

~

Nothing more infuriating than a
deaf old man pretending to be hearing.

If you're a mile wide and an inch deep, you need to
keep changing the subject.

~

It's good to be accommodating but
not good to be a doormat.

~

Always trust that small voice in your head
when it says, "Shut up, you idiot!"

~

When half the guests have
gone home, be among them.

~

Good manners can be taught, but not the warmth
of spirit that gives them meaning.

~

Making faces is like having the contents
of your brain projected onto a screen.

Try not to mistake shyness for unfriendliness.

❧

No, I do not want a piece of your mind,
but thanks for the offer.

❧

A good host makes every guest feel special —
if only for a moment.

❧

There are ways in which it is good for
an adult to be childlike, but none in
which it is good to be childish.

❧

Sometimes the mouth tells one story,
and the rest of the face tells another.

❧

Why would someone answer
the phone saying, "I can't talk now?"

Gossips are like radio stations—
because the things they hear are
first amplified, and then broadcast.

Suprisingly there are people who go
through their entire lives without
ever being wrong about anything.

A party is more interesting if you
talk to the people you don't know.

Anything you say and do in a rage
is carved in stone.

Marriage & Family

*T*eenage girls converse at
the speed of light.

~

The problem for would-be matchmakers is that
while common interests are easy to find,
attraction remains the great mystery.

~

The smartest and the dumbest kids
get into trouble, but the smart ones
pass through the trouble.

~

Your early years were a series
of experiments in managing adults.

~

Does a man finally understand
women after his sex change?

You can do a lot of leaving in your life but
all your baggage follows.

～

The art of listening should be taught
in all schools, because few will learn it at home.

～

I'll just keep saying it until you
get tired of not hearing it.

～

If your little boy is never bad, you should seek
professional help as soon as possible.

～

In a flash, rage transforms beauty
into a hideous mask.

～

Two poor listeners can be happy together,
as neither expects to be heard.

They kept their unhappy marriage
together for the sake of the children—
because that's what their parents did.

~

Seated at the farthest table with the distant
cousins and the ex-neighbors, you feel
like you barely made the cut.

~

You know how to push buttons in your family—
and what happens when you do—
so why do you keep pushing those buttons?

~

Lacking the ability to express our feelings,
we validate certain occasions by
spending a lot of money.

~

A marriage that goes on the rocks
can still take a long time to sink.

Placing all your hopes on
your children is a very risky bet.

～

If you have any sense, your concept
of what is sexy ages as you do.

～

A family has a way of simply forgetting the
existence of a difficult and angry relative.

～

When you have small children,
ten percent of your life is personal.

～

Dysfunctional is repeating behavior
that didn't work the first time.

～

There are people whose lives are ruined
if they never have children, and others
whose lives are ruined if they do.

A common misconception is that
your family is crazier than most.

∾

Not honoring your parents is
dishonoring yourself.

∾

Unconditional love from your parents
is a very good start in life, but few
are lucky enough to get it.

∾

It is the egg that chooses the sperm, and takes her
time about it—and this is how men learn to wait.

∾

Parents don't like their parents
telling them how to parent.

∾

You must decipher the rules of the
family that you marry into.

In marriage, it is better to be wrong because
being right is the right to remain celibate.

Children want nothing more than they
want their parents to love each other.

Women look for husbands far more
than men look for wives.

The histories of most families are
writ in a garage full of junk.

I have six billion cousins, but I am only on
speaking terms with a few hundred of them.

Don't forget that family stories
are mostly just stories.

Finding just the right gift is a gift.

~

Dating is fun until you start doing it with
intentions—then it becomes nerve-wracking.

~

Just the sight of a happy family is therapeutic.

~

The worst part of divorce is knowing that
you will have to go through dating again.

~

An unhappy marriage is already a separation.

~

There is nothing more embarrassing to a teenager
than having parents and being seen with them.

~

Resentment is one of the privileges of privilege.

You can blame your parents for your childhood,
but don't blame them for your adulthood.

≈

It's a lot easier to start a family feud
than to stop one.

≈

Have you ever heard a father telling his thirty-year-
old son, "I'm worried that you aren't married yet"?

≈

Monogamy often flourishes when
the field has been sown with wild oats.

≈

She only wanted to marry money and
that's why money did not want to marry her.

≈

The only thing that is seldom contested
in a divorce is the wedding album.

The course that is a mandatory prerequisite to
all further education is called Toilet Training.

≈

If you are a good parent your children will
make their own mistakes, but not yours.

≈

My kids have difficulties; other people's
kids have problems.

≈

Our obligations to our children
are reversed in old age.

≈

Relationships built on obligation
are always grudging.

≈

Your parents didn't think you had any sense,
and theirs felt the same way about them.

With marriage, sometimes it
takes a few tries to get it right.

~

It's the thought that counts, but
a thoughtful present counts more.

~

Let your parents come to live with you,
but never go to live with your parents.

~

Before responding to provocation,
take a breath and count to a thousand.

~

Look at this terrible wound I have made
out of a small slight!

~

Ninety-eight percent of social engagements
are arranged by wives, the other
two percent are unaccounted for.

To find the right person, become the right person.

∽

Sometimes even an adult needs
to be told when to go to bed.

∽

Sometimes the opposite of no is still no.

∽

The intimacies of a Wednesday-night poker game
can outlast those of the player's marriages.

∽

Pray to a saint, but never marry one.

∽

After a certain age all the single men
seem to disappear.

∽

The most complicated of all contracts
is the marriage contract.

Babies do not negotiate.

∾

One job, one house, one wife—
believe it or not, it does happen.

∾

The youngest child wears the oldest clothes.

∾

A happy family is of little interest to novelists,
psychologists, or other experts in dysfunction.

∾

The latest form of child abuse is heavy scheduling.

∾

The child whose needs are unmet becomes the
adult whose needs can never be met.

∾

"Make Love, Not War," sounded
pretty good to me, so I did.

We must learn to walk on our own twice.

A man stays in touch with society
by means of a wife.

Marry someone who reads instructions.

The most incompetent of parents began
their work by producing a perfect baby.

We do not practice equal opportunity forgiveness.

As a marriage matures, the number of
understandings, agreements, and treaties
multiplies, as between nations at peace.

Memory

We worry about losing our memory,
yet there are things we wish we
could forget.

∾

Share your thoughts, not your memoirs.

∾

As adults we remember far more than
ever happened during our childhood.

∾

The great joy of an old-timer is telling
a newcomer how great it was twenty years ago.

∾

Some people have names that are hard to
remember, and others have faces that are hard
to remember—and a few have names and
faces that are impossible to remember.

Who cares what you did twenty years ago?
What matters is what you are doing now.

≈

Photos and memories can be
retouched to make them prettier.

≈

I pride myself on my memory—
that vast warehouse of trivia.

≈

There are people who tell the story of their life
over and over again until they come to believe it.

≈

My childhood memories of the verdant smells of
nature are more vivid than anything my nose
is able to detect now.

≈

A chess master has a tremendous gift
that is perfectly useless.

Don't schlep your past everywhere.

≈

If you can remember the names and faces of a
thousand people you are presidential timber.

≈

You can't build memories out of daydreams.

≈

I had a great idea while shaving,
but I forgot it as I rinsed my face.

≈

Everything was amazing when I was little, but
each year it grew a little less so—yet when I recall
my amazement, or see it reflected in the face of
a child, I am again in touch with the absolute
amazingness of everything in this world.

≈

The reason that I am standing here in the garage
is probably that I was going to get something.

There is something scary about a friend who
remembers everything you ever said or did.

≈

Looking back over your life you will discover
that the easiest moments to recall are
first times and last times.

≈

Memory is a huge cave in which
you have only a tiny candle.

≈

Leave the sleeping dogs
of your past to their slumbers.

≈

You are never really alone with your thoughts,
because so many voices and faces crowd into them.

≈

A tattoo is a way of keeping alive the
memory of being young and stupid.

Those who have taken a walk on the wild side in
their youth have a certain gleam in their eyes.

~

The mind travels most smoothly in well-worn ruts.

~

When it becomes possible to Google my brain,
I'll stop worrying about Alzheimer's.

~

In a desk drawer lie your mystery keys—
you have no idea what they are for, but are
afraid to throw them away, just in case.

~

The missing part of my brain is called a list—
and I'd better be holding it in my hand
when I get to the store.

~

It's reassuring to see other people
looking for their cars in parking lots.

Morality

*T*he echo of crime is the slamming
of a prison-cell door.

~

A martyr is someone who throws his
life away for something you believe in.

~

Human nature is, for most purposes, only the
nature of the people you allow into your life.

~

There was once a distinction
between famous and infamous.

~

Most of us would rather lose the
manuscript of our entire past than
have certain chapters published.

The most skillful liar is one who is able to
persuade himself of the truth of his lie.

∼

To avoid complications, tell the truth
or change the subject.

∼

Morality is like quicksand:
one sinks more easily than one rises.

∼

A skillful liar begins with the truth
and then works in tints and shadings.

∼

More loose behavior is prevented by the
fear of gossip than by morality, law,
and religion combined.

∼

Poor people go to jail from rage,
rich people from greed.

A public defender is hardly defending the public.

~

There is about the same amount of depravity
everywhere—the only difference being that
there are places in which it is on display.

~

It takes character to be a good poker
player—deceitful, calculating, and
secretive character.

~

The finger of blame points
outward in all directions.

~

We flaunt our little sins, like a weakness for
sweets, and keep the big ones to ourselves.

~

Nature gives children personalities;
parents give them values.

The truth is always the simple version.

≈

We go through life hearing few lies—
but plenty of the truth being bent, filtered,
retouched, twisted, shaded, and massaged.

≈

The mentality of criminals is
so contagious it infects even the police.

≈

You have only to be caught in a single lie
to become known as a liar.

≈

Half of police work is a stupid treasure hunt
for bags of useless powders and weeds.

≈

You should devote ten seconds a day to
worrying about what other people will think.

A prude is generally a very dirty-minded person.

~

You may ask what is the right thing to do,
but in your heart you already know.

~

Moral authority is the hardest kind
of authority to acquire.

~

Never tell someone at a reunion that they must
remember you—because that forces them
to pretend they do.

~

Avoid people who are always right—
unless you enjoy always being wrong.

~

Charisma blinds our eyes to the
completely fraudulent.

That your great-great grandfather
was a horse thief is amusing—
that your father was an embezzler is not.

The most effective truth serum is 80 proof.

Having to reply to an uncomfortable question
doesn't mean that you have to reply to *that
particular* uncomfortable question.

The main opportunities for people of poor
character come from finding people
who are poor judges of character.

The simple truth is the only kind there is.

Nature

*I*n California we expect nature to
periodically kick our butts.

∿

It was awkward learning to stand on our hind legs,
but after only two million years, we are able to
operate computers with our front paws.

∿

We rule nature, but we are ruled by our natures.

∿

The landscape of your childhood is
the one that is most real to you.

∿

Accepting an invitation for a sail is like
going to a party that you aren't allowed
to leave until the host decides it's over.

Mankind is warlike because we are all descended from fierce warriors—if they had not been fierce, our ancestors would not have survived.

～

There is no landscape made by man that surpasses any landscape not made by man.

～

Humans are the only species that can love another species more than their own.

～

An ant doesn't look like it knows where it's going, but it does.

～

Country people seldom say that they are looking forward to getting away to the city for a weekend.

～

Being in nature is very tiring— afterwards I must have a long nap.

A forest makes a very good neighbor.

Nature is always beautiful if you are a
human—the rest of creation is looking
for other creatures to eat.

If I were my cat I would know what I want in life.

In the history of the earth, anything
that lives on land is a newcomer.

A cat has boundaries.

My backyard is wilderness enough.

A tree makes a good living on
water and carbon dioxide.

As the top predator, we have the luxury of being
able to linger over the carcass at our dinner.

❦

Naturally, I tried hard to be natural,
but it's not my nature.

❦

The next age of mankind will be
the Age of Consequences.

❦

The Gray-haired Woman has
become an endangered species.

❦

An environmentalist in the boardroom
is worth two in the bush.

❦

A dog has just enough consciousness
to be anxious.

The herring can no more conceive that it is
going to be pickled in a jar than we can
conceive that we are made out of herring.

≈

If you really considered what is involved
in walking on two legs you would hardly
be able to stand up.

≈

Global warming is global karma.

≈

Nothing is possible
that goes against human nature.

≈

When you have poison oak
you love nature a little less.

≈

In our own backyards, we are all NIMBYs.

It is impossible to swim in the ocean
without thinking of *Jaws*.

∾

From the viewpoint of a fly,
a human is most useful when dead.

∾

As a bird hunts twigs for her nest,
so we head for the home center.

∾

Four tons of automobiles in your driveway,
and you talk about the environment?

∾

Bird watchers and hunters occasionally meet in
the woods, but they have little to talk about.

∾

The art of camping is making do
without what you forgot to bring.

Your dog is not adorable if it's in the habit
of sticking its nose in people's crotches.

~

Nature always finds ways to
limit a population—as it will our own.

~

Birds teach us to keep our eyes open.

~

The stoic character supposedly created
by harsh winters is actually a symptom
of seasonal depression.

~

A garden is a state of unnatural nature.

~

Farming is a partnership between man and nature
in which nature is the majority partner.

We are an invasive species.

Watching my fingers moving over this
keyboard, they resemble the legs
of a crab roaming the sea floor.

Once, we all got everything we needed by crying.

A wilderness trail is a freeway for backpackers,
loaded like pack mules with granola and gadgets.

A cat has an entire beauty salon in her tongue.

Politics

A government that is not feared could not collect enough taxes to make a living for itself.

≈

Ten dollars an hour on one side of the fence,
ten dollars a day on the other—
would the fence stop you?

≈

The budget is always cut so as to cause
the most pain, in order to reconcile
the citizens to the next tax increase.

≈

Politicians are the hand puppets
of their speechwriters.

≈

A three-year-old snatches a toy from his playmate,
and this is the beginning of imperialism.

There are an infinite number of societies in any
society, and they can barely conceive of each other.

~

The armies of democracies
tend to hold their ground.

~

Compared to the behavior of nations,
I declare myself sane.

~

To improve your wind for running,
pretend that you are a politician.

~

If it is very good or very bad,
it probably originated in California.

~

The leftist has chosen a marginal life on the
fringes of society, and viewing society from that
fringe, he produces a cockeyed critique of it.

The efficiency of a government agency
can be too small to measure.

~

I have arranged the map of the world
to keep my coffee cup and my gas tank full.

~

Politics is a much rougher game than football.

~

We like the police to be handy—but not too close.

~

Discuss politics only with people who always vote.

~

A government that doesn't provide healthcare
for its citizens is hardly worth the price.

~

A nation of homeowners is more concerned
with lawns than with politics.

One begins a legal dispute with
an irrational belief in justice.

～

What was thought to be a conspiracy usually
turns out to be a major instance of stupidity.

～

Congress tends to resemble itself more
than it resembles the country.

～

In politics, as in ancient Rome,
the knife is still placed in the back.

～

I have not encountered any form of taxation
that comes with representation.

～

Everyone who sees action in war
is to some extent a casualty.

Nonviolence works well against pacifists.

∼

The left always venerates the working class,
a love that is seldom reciprocated.

∼

The American brain is not sufficiently evolved
to grasp the duplicities of the Middle East.

∼

The preppie millionaire is coached to speak
like a workin' man when he runs for office.

∼

"One nation, indivisible" — except by race,
ethnicity, region, politics, class,
religion, age, and gender.

∼

The Constitution is mostly a matter
of interpretation, like the Bible.

Majorities are generally not too fond of minorities.

∾

Military discipline enables an army facing a
superior enemy to contemplate its impending
destruction with equanimity.

∾

We are taught to believe in our
system of government, whatever that is.

∾

It is best not to come to the attention
of the government.

∾

God may be on our side, but He is not
always in a mood to play.

∾

Would you listen to a radio station
that reported only good news?

Our faith in democracy is shaken
by the election of a complete fool.

∾

Medals are given only for murders
committed in uniform.

∾

Your legal lifestyle rests comfortably
on the shoulders of illegal immigrants.

∾

The Right hates minorities
and the Left hates the country.

∾

I can't say I have much to show
for my lifetime of voting.

∾

No one is entitled to anything more
than a decent opportunity.

It takes a lot of money getting elected to
the Senate, but there is even more
money in being an ex-senator.

～

Because we find people more interesting
than ideas or events, we can hardly blame the
media for a shallow focus on personalities.

～

The price of freedom is blood, but not
the blood of those who arranged the transaction.

～

What normal person would seek high office?

～

When charisma enters the room,
common sense goes out the window.

～

The oppressed peoples of the world long for
democracy—but not for our kind of democracy.

A white person has no defense against
a charge of unconscious racism.

A political party does the least
for a constituency it has in its pocket.

Fervently believing that you're a
victim of injustice is about the same
as actually being a victim of injustice.

It is unfair that polls influence elections,
even when they're wrong.

Can you tell where the news ends
and the propaganda begins?

A well-regulated militia would not
enlist paranoid gun nuts.

Absolute certainty is the privilege of fanatics.

In the military you learn how to follow orders
exactly, including those that will make you dead.

As their cities were being leveled,
the Germans began to grasp the
fundamental errors of Nazi thought.

In the perfect bureaucracy,
the buck stops nowhere.

The minority cannot but feel wronged
when the majority is an ass.

When the presidential couple go to bed,
a Secret Service agent is always stationed at
their bedroom door—not listening, of course.

The basic idea of an army is that you can
kill people without murdering them.

~

The intelligence, of a government that both admits
and justifies torture is somewhat open to question.

~

A public figure with even half a brain says
absolutely nothing "off the record."

~

One more word about conspiracies
and you're on my list of airheads.

~

Extremists think in historical terms more than
most people—but only to confirm their prejudices.

~

We go to war to preserve our way of life—
a way of life featuring a strong military
and a readiness to go to war.

Protest demonstrations validate the importance of their leaders—by proving that they have followers.

The President of the United States—
our disposable monarch.

Paranoia is the default mentality
of the far left and the far right.

We were told we were winning the Vietnam War
until the last Americans were helicoptered
off the roof of the embassy.

Religion

After my enlightenment—
ask me then.

~

The prayers of an atheist
have a special charm to God.

~

There is often a moment in a sermon when
the preacher looks like he's not sure where
he is going with what he is saying.

~

One spark can burn a forest—
one divine spark can transform a life.

~

Money can easily be raised to build a
magnificent house of worship; filling it with
worshipers is a more difficult matter.

It was a great sermon—
I stayed awake almost until the end.

∾

Faith in religion is possible just as arithmetic
exists and is useful, even though numbers
are entirely imagined.

∾

Anyone who has a conception
of God is a theologian.

∾

I'll be happy to see anyone,
assuming there is an afterlife.

∾

The problem of evil sticks in the
craw of religion like a fishbone.

∾

The leaders of all great religions have but
one thing in common: funny hats.

Fundamentalists and scientists agree that
the world is coming to an end, their only
difference being seven billion years.

~

If you like to take chances with your faith,
ask your spiritual leader a political question.

~

I climbed a mountain and I saw God—
or could it have been the altitude?

~

Religion reminds us that we
can be better than we are.

~

A religion can run on even ten percent faith.

~

In a hundred years there will be a world culture,
and in a thousand years there will be a world race,
but there will never be one world religion.

If you would like your prayers to be granted,
pray that you should become a better person.

≈

I would cast plenty of stones,
if only I were without sin.

≈

God's idea of hilarious would be
a conversation with a theologian.

≈

Safer to put your faith in religion
than in the stock market.

≈

Leviticus is no fun.

≈

There is no limit to the
spiritual wealth you can acquire.

Globalization is bad news for local gods.

～

New-Age people do not have
anything exactly in mind.

～

At a silent retreat I discovered
that I really didn't have much to say.

～

God chuckles at ten seconds of blasphemy
when you whack your thumb with a hammer.

～

Religion is a marketplace of wisdom and values,
and only what is useful deserves to survive.

～

Heaven is a place where
there is plenty of work to do.

The miracle is that I'm as
religious as I am, considering the atheism.

≈

Step one of becoming a guru is
downloading a lot of wisdom.

≈

The Bible is tribal.

≈

Through meditation I have discovered
that I am my mind's slave.

≈

Religion will outlast any belief in the supernatural.

≈

If the answer to any spiritual question is readily
provided, you are in the presence of a charlatan.

God created man in His image—then He got
really busy and created 950,000 species of insects.

❧

The Jews have ten thousand popes, all infallible.

❧

Fully observing any religion would
leave little time for anything else.

❧

If there were no organized religions
we could all be one religion.

❧

A religion may be ecumenical,
but it does not like to share its followers.

❧

Behave as if the fly on the wall were God.

Has anyone noticed that the Crusades
occur every thousand years?

In a hundred years there will be a world culture,
and in a thousand years there will be a world race,
but there will never be one world religion.

Science & Technology

*E*very day of my life, a major discovery.

~

God-fearing man is being replaced
by Science-fearing man.

~

Physics is becoming more improbable
than religion.

~

The human mind is more like a kaleidoscope
than a microscope or a telescope.

~

Gravity gets me down.

~

Sometimes a mere probability is
promoted to a proof.

I was born in the Atomic Age
and I will die in the Technology Age.

~

All we see is the skin of the onion.

~

If someone has a new idea and you
instantly offer an objection, you are
part of the problem, not the solution.

~

More problems are solved by tinkering
than by brilliance.

~

Thanks to rapid advances in technology,
for the first time in history we are no longer
able to fix anything.

~

Most problems are manageable if you
can just think of something to try.

If you enjoy banging your head on your desk,
I suggest not backing up your computer files.

❧

Psychology proves the danger of applying
theories about human nature to real life.

❧

Economists can now predict the past
with great accuracy.

❧

Open a bag of your favorite potato chips
and you will begin to believe in the
concept of perpetual motion.

❧

A genius is someone who has had at least
one truly original thought during his lifetime.

❧

Freud left a fog over psychology that is just
beginning to lift; Jung left a primordial swamp.

What Hegel and Marx called the dialectic
is actually the mind of a neurotic, in which
everything calls up its opposite and a negation.

∾

In the final struggle,
we will not rule nature, nature will rule us.

∾

Technology enables us to always
be in touch without ever touching.

∾

Breaking up requires a lot of deleting.

∾

Our brains are running software
that is two million years old.

∾

We live in the Age of Technology—
but most of us don't have a clue.

Science and technology are at work
against democracy as they deliver increasingly
sophisticated means of manipulating
a confused electorate.

≈

Just you and me—and the phone, our cell phones,
radio, TV, Internet, and the thousand
things that are on our minds.

≈

The ultimate thing to be feared from technology
is a time when thoughts are no longer private.

≈

We Americans have an advantage in technology
because in many countries an educated person
would never touch a tool.

≈

The toothpaste is never empty,
we just get tired of squeezing the tube.

Technology is burying us in new features.

~

I had a nightmare in which my life was ruined
because I had forgotten all my passwords.

~

Assembly instructions are written by gremlins.

~

The difference between a brilliant inventor
and a brilliant crackpot is the filter.

~

As technology continues to reduce our attention
span from minutes to seconds to fractions of a
second, it becomes difficult to communicate any
thought that cannot be grasped in a few words.

~

The Internet is a city in which a
bad neighborhood can appear on any corner.

The command on your computer
that could destroy your life is called send.

~

In ideas, size matters.

~

Information junkies are beginning
to die from overdoses.

~

The word "repair" has been
replaced by the word "replace."

~

They laugh in the face of gravity—
those engineers of skyscrapers, bridges,
and brassieres.

~

If we had decent fur we might not
have invented fire.

We share ninety-seven percent of our genes with
chimpanzees—I treasure the other three percent.

~

Never rule out the highly improbable; it is
possible, for example, that a very tall woman in
high heels in a gay bar is actually a woman.

~

The lands of the world are mostly empty,
because humans tend to swarm.

~

Walking into a lamp post while texting
is an instant message from reality.

~

The Internet allows you to have the illusion
that by interacting, you are acting.

~

Regarding all of humanity's future plans, all bets
are off due to the randomness of the universe.

Densely written jargon is a method
scholars use to disguise a lack of content.

≈

If you are a mosquito, the great mystery
of the universe is mosquito repellent.

≈

The word "proven" belongs more
to marketing than to science.

≈

From the viewpoint of a virus that lives twenty
minutes, we are almost immortal,
yet the virus can kill us.

≈

Science is an idea that married a grant
and gave birth to a discovery.

≈

Taking everything into consideration—
it would be impossible to ever make a decision.

We are losing the war against microbes because
their adaptability trumps our intelligence.

∾

We no longer know if the consumers drive the
technology or the technology
drives the consumers.

∾

The best arguments against the theory
of evolution are the brains of the
fundamentalists who reject it.

∾

Unlikely coincidences occur frequently because
the number of things that could occur is
practically infinite.

∾

We know that we don't understand the science
behind the computer on our desk, but actually
we don't even understand the desk.

We are constantly seeking explanations,
but many things are the way they are
for no particular reason.

Due to Heisenberg's uncertainty principle,
a small object, when dropped, will roll farther
away than seems possible and then disappear.

Time

I just noticed that I got old,
right after I was young.

~

There is so much to do, and we only
have a moment out of eternity....

~

The older you get, the fewer excuses you need.

~

There is no time and place more interesting
than the time and place you are at now.

~

The hardest thing to do gracefully is age.

~

At what age does one discover that it is
possible to sit quietly?

I'm too old to argue.

≈

Today you have a day less than you had
yesterday—did you spend it wisely?

≈

An hour is not so long—neither is a lifetime.

≈

To have a sense of history is to know how
quickly one's generation slips into oblivion.

≈

It is our oldest feature that betrays our real age.

≈

All good things must come to an end—
but not all mediocre things.

≈

"Ageless" is a nice way of saying really, really old.

What is written in stone will be erased by geology.

~

Thirty years ago I could do cartwheels—
now I can do mental ones.

~

Passing a mirror…"who is that weird old person"?

~

If you still have all the ideals of your youth forty
years later, you are probably some kind of nut.

~

Your past is not an excuse for your present.

~

If you wish to call attention to your age,
complain about all your aches and pains.

~

Curmudgeons do not improve with age.

The little bit of time we have on earth
is precious—yet we can only relax
by wasting some of it.

≈

All news is old news, tomorrow.

≈

By the time most people get any money sense,
it's too late for them to get any money.

≈

I was bored in school because they taught
everything the long way.

≈

It takes a strong optimist to face
old age cheerfully, but there are many who do.

≈

True success is not having to
account for your time to anyone.

For my grandchildren to know that their grandfather was a hippie is like me knowing that my grandmother was a flapper and that her grandmother was a Bloomer girl.

~

Busyness wastes more of life than idleness.

~

When you get old you will look like an owl—but with large glasses you can look like a wise owl.

~

In the dream world everything is at the same time, and everywhere is right next to everywhere else.

~

Time is not on anyone's side.

~

A few minutes in a doctor's waiting room is about an hour.

Just when you get used to being a certain age,
another damn birthday comes along.

～

There is an age at which one discovers that
one has a lifetime supply of certain items.

～

I love to watch a beautiful sunset—and I have
heard that a sunrise is pretty good too.

～

If you are well fed, and you get old,
eventually you will look like an owl.

～

There is no beauty greater than graceful old age.

～

I have a lot of mileage on me—am I entitled
to an upgrade on my life journey?

The older people get, the more
they have in common.

～

Why do I waste time? Because it can' be recycled.

～

It is not true that everyone has the same
amount of time—some people have more
time in an hour than others have in a week.

～

Tomorrow is far more interesting than yesterday.

～

One day is like another, and yet each day
unfolds with its own unique logic.

～

We never lack fraudulent reasons for
putting off things we should be doing.

The coins in your pocket are a remnant
of life in the ancient world.

~

Don't tell me what I should have done
differently, I'm no time traveler.

~

Really nice people generally have
time to stop and visit—it seems that the universe
allots them more time.

❧

Vanity

A movie-star-quality facelift is
so good it almost fools you.

～

You can't make up stories for
the people who read you like a book.

～

The most useful volunteers
will do anything except serve on a board.

～

Men will notice a short skirt more
than a tastefully chosen outfit.

～

The great talent of a narcissist is a knack for
turning any subject, no matter how unrelated,
into something about himself.

Young people must pose because
they don't know what they are yet.

≈

The flunky must prove his status by
being more arrogant than the master.

≈

Better to remain unknown than
to have once been famous.

≈

If you have a fear of being boring,
just keep people talking about themselves.

≈

You say that you aren't vain—
so try going an entire day without saying "I".

≈

We ask the mirror not if we are the fairest in
the land, but if we are still even a little bit sexy.

If you had to write down ten totally honest
statements describing your personality, would
you be willing to share them with anyone?

≈

Money and sex—the bricks and mortar
of our fantasy lives.

≈

A "good editorial" is one that states
the opinion we already held.

≈

We are all the stars of our own reality shows.

≈

My opinion of myself reaches a low when I
bite my tongue severely while eating a sandwich.

≈

Honestly, suppose you had to choose
between becoming sexier or becoming smarter?

Better to get up and dance badly than
to sit and watch the dancing.

~

I'm planning to enter a liar's contest
and tell this short, but sure-fire winner:
"I have absolutely no regrets in my life."

~

We prefer to believe that others think well of us,
because the alternative is too unpleasant to consider.

~

How strange that a few hundred years ago
men displayed their legs in silk stockings
while women concealed theirs….

~

We score some cheap easy virtue by
giving change to a homeless person, recycling
a little plastic pill bottle, or doing a few
minutes of halfhearted exercise.

The one place we do not enjoy seeing
our reflection is in the pupils of our dentist.

∾

Ask a few leading questions and
most people will tell you everything.

∾

We prefer the natural over the artificial,
except when the natural is unflattering.

∾

There's nothing wrong with being eccentric if
you're an English lord with plenty of money—
otherwise, you should keep it under control.

∾

To be vain, first pretend that you are attractive.

∾

An important person vanishes,
consumed by his own importance.

Vain does not see vanity.

∼

If you think your possessions are valuable,
try holding a yard sale.

∼

There are no immortal words.

∼

I am extremely proud of my humility
and my modesty.

∼

There is no beauty with a sour expression.

∼

We like to believe that we are
better looking than our photos.

∼

An oversized ego is like tight pants on a big butt.

Vanity is more durable than beauty.

≈

Try not to frown when you
are considering something.

≈

As we fuss over a tiny spot on our pants,
somewhere in a very poor country a man is
attempting to cover his nakedness with a
tattered rag that once was pants.

≈

Don't brag about your possessions,
they are only yours for a little while.

≈

Give that aging sexpot lots of credit for trying.

≈

How could you have ever thought that I actually
wanted your honest opinion of how I look?

Now that you are famous—so what?

If our egos were our skins there would
be scars on the scar tissue.

As gravity pulls you to the earth,
so vanity pulls you to the mirror.

An improvement in the manufacture of mirrors
is also an advancement in vanity.

We find our own skin more fascinating
than any abstract painting.

Forty years of feminism—
and still those stupid shoes.

Wealth

*I*n a country lacking an aristocracy,
money does the job nicely.

≈

It is always a good time to invest in kindness.

≈

If you are wondering if you can afford something,
you probably can't.

≈

Much more pleasant to buy things than
to try to make a living selling them.

≈

Money is like water: it seeks its own level;
we are most comfortable with those who have
about the same amount of it as we do.

What you own lets you sleep—
what you owe keeps you up at night.

~

He bragged about the stock that doubled,
but forgot to mention the one that halved.

~

The rise and fall of the economy is a
force of nature that central bankers
and economists pretend to manage.

~

If you have money at the end of a business career,
you are never really sure if it is due to your skill
and wisdom, or to the dumb luck of having
been in the right place at the right time.

~

When investors get greedy, that is
when the serious money is lost.

I wish I had a dollar for every dollar I ever had.

～

Economies worked well enough
before there were economists.

～

In the locker room you hear smart opinions
about sports and dumb ones about investments.

～

When we say that they have money, or that they
don't have money, we are really saying that they
have more or less money than we have.

～

A nation of debtors is not a free people.

～

Alchemy didn't disappear, it was
transmuted into economics.

The Christians must shop fervently at Christmas,
or God will smite the economy.

❧

How appropriate that a nation of debtors should
be ruled by a government that runs on debt.

❧

To the poor, interest is something that you pay;
for the wealthy it is something that you collect.

❧

In a wealthy country the rich are thinner than the
poor; in a very poor country it is the reverse.

❧

A trip to Las Vegas is a bet against the house.

❧

If you want to waste your life, believe that making
a lot of money is going to make you happy.

Never complain about the price of something
you bought—it was worth that price because
some fool was willing to pay it.

∾

The less you want, the less you need;
the more you want, the more you need.

∾

In very backward countries people foolishly believe
that being with family and friends
is more important than money.

∾

The real poor complain very little,
as they expect nothing.

∾

For every billionaire there are a thousand
millionaires, and for every millionaire
there are a thousand thousandaires.

A contradiction of capitalism is that
it depends on both saving and spending.

~

Easy credit in our materialistic society
has reduced many to a state of bondage
enforced by the laws of the nation.

~

Investing is always a gamble,
but gamblers make poor investors.

~

When the economy crashes, you need to keep
your head, even if you've lost everything else.

~

The mark of an amateur investor
is believing in a stock.

~

Most people have too much credit
for their own wealth.

Most wealth has been reduced to numbers on a
monthly statement—it has no other real existence
than in the belief systems of capitalism.

❦

How long will I have to work to pay
for this thing I am about to buy?

❦

If you really know money, it will come to you,
in good times or bad.

❦

Would a dog work like a dog to pay
for a bigger doghouse?

❦

I followed all the rules—so where is the money?

❦

Business is largely an exchange of money
between people who were born to make it
and people who were born to lose it.

Suppose you could be twice as rich but
it took half your life to get there?

≈

Poverty appreciates everything—
wealth only the best.

≈

Shopping is like sex, in that desires
are aroused and then satisfied.

≈

In America we save empty jars, grocery bags,
redwoods, whales, the planet—
everything but money.

≈

Casinos are organized on the principle that people
wish to lose their money as efficiently as possible.

≈

Heaven would be filled with big tippers
if God were a waitress.

The only difference between the amateur and the
professional investor is that the amateur
buys at the peak and sells at the bottom.

～

The laws of economics are continually
being rewritten by human ingenuity.

～

Just think of where we might be now if only we
had blah, blah, blah when blah, blah, blah ....

～

New money can't bear anything
that is even slightly shabby.

～

We never tire of reading of millionaires
who are sent to jail.

～

People who are born to make money
understand economics better than any economist.

People who are competent with their money
worry the most, and people who are
incompetent with it worry the least.

~

A real man knows how to fix anything,
but a wimp knows how to make a lot of
money to hire people to fix anything.

~

The hateful thing about insurance
is that something bad has to happen for you
to get any value from it.

~

The immigrant who fails to learn the language is
money in the bank for his countryman who does.

~

The rich keep busy because they
fear being seen as idle.

Cheap money is for sale to the rich
and expensive money is for sale to the poor.

If we'd known then what we know now,
we would all be millionaires.

Spending all your money during your lifetime
is like being your own heir.

If you are wealthy money is like the air;
if you are poor it is like the moon.

Wisdom

*T*he best advice I can give you is
to learn to take good advice.

~

A pig is much smarter than a pigheaded person.

~

Are you really sure you know
what it feels like to be an idiot?

~

We would rather give good advice than take it.

~

A university is a place in which thought
is neatly compartmentalized.

~

You can't take bullshit by the horns.

I have a hundred things
on my mind and not much in it.

~

Original thinkers are irritating because they insert
a grain of sand under the shell of our complacency.

~

Don't expect a keen exchange of opinion
with someone who has a dull ax to grind.

~

Let me think about that for…a few years.

~

An authority on everything is
an authority on nothing.

~

If you could sum up everything you've learned,
and then subtract everything you're not
sure about, what would the remainder be?

That's my opinion, I read it somewhere.

≈

The wisdom of the ages is sitting on a barstool, but the future is being mapped in a coffeehouse.

≈

What was I thinking when I was so thoughtless?

≈

Given the choice, how many men would choose a very large brain and a very small penis over a very small brain and a very large penis?

≈

There is no school of philosophy that approaches ordinary common sense.

≈

Scholarship assumes that the true facts are always complicated— common sense assumes that they aren't.

That's what I said, but not what I meant,
such is my poverty of language.

～

A person who is generally miserable
can still become a great philosopher.

～

You don't have to be a great thinker
to be a thoughtful person.

～

First thought, best thought—
last thought, also best thought.

～

Now that I am old and wise
I might learn something.

～

Sometimes we turn on the radio because silence
would leave us alone with our troubled thoughts.

People often elevate mere prejudices
to "a philosophy."

∾

Some people learn everything they need to know
in kindergarten, others in traffic school.

∾

An expert is a person who is incapable
of being wrong about a certain subject.

∾

If you have thought about the issues and formed
your own opinion you are equal to any pundit.

∾

Like a bee that buzzes from flower to flower,
the mind buzzes from thought to thought.

∾

The good teacher always has a smart class and the
bad teacher always has a dumb one.

There is dumb and dumber, but no dumbest.

~

Awareness ebbs and flows
as we drift through our day.

~

A man of few words might also
be a man of few thoughts.

~

Put your helmet on before you start
banging your head on the wall.

~

Relying on luck is the plan of many,
but it is not a very good plan.

~

If you don't think you've made a lot of
mistakes in your life, you've learned nothing.

There is a thoughtful place—
located midway between the extremes.

∿

Only call yourself stupid.

∿

Professors talk as if ideas could exist
in the world without context.

∿

The insight can be brilliant without being
completely true in all circumstances.

∿

A reliable method of simulating wisdom
is cryptic muttering.

∿

In a very quiet place there is only the
clamor of your thoughts.

It seemed almost as if one day I was young and stupid, and the next I was old and wise.

～

You can't fit large ideas into small minds.

～

An intellectual tends to see complexities where they do not actually exist.

～

We must raise our consciousness while lowering our self-consciousness.

～

If you consider every aspect of life a problem to be considered, you might just be a philosopher.

～

You can't argue with simple matters of fact, but people do it all the time.

The ideal liberal arts education would develop
intellectuals who don't intellectualize.

≈

When we meet an original thinker
our complacency is shaken.

≈

Hone your ideas; grind them to a fine edge.

≈

People who know nothing
are the first to say, "I know."

≈

If you would just reverse that opinion slightly I
would be in complete agreement with you.

≈

We are only passengers driven
by our restless minds.

I forgive all my teachers for what I don't know.

∾

Wise men are often to be found at home,
the world having no use for them.

∾

This world is far more interesting than anything
that could happen merely inside my head.

∾

I am contemplating my navel,
and find it rather deep.

∾

It must be consoling to be a philosopher,
when things go wrong in your life.

∾

If I were an ant, the grain of salt with which
I take your opinion would be a boulder.

I am pretty sure that I am right about something.

～

Gaining control of your thoughts is as easy as
sitting by the ocean and controlling the waves.

～

Because I am a genius,
I only need to use half my wit.

～

Real ideas have exactness,
but nonsense is always vague.

～

If you really have something to say,
plain language will do.

～

Philosophy is about how to live, but the lives of the
great philosophers provide few useful role models.

The mind can also become constipated.

Most of what is useful in life is known
only to a small minority of alert listeners.

The heart is the most intelligent organ.

Don't give advice without first
asking if advice is wanted.

It isn't possible to be an angry philosopher.

Work

_J_ust try, in your life, to do one
thing really, really well.

~

Creative excuses show imagination—but those
who offer them were seldom hired
for their imagination.

~

There are times when you must ignore everyone
around you if you are to get anything done—
but these situations only occur about twice a day.

~

From den mother to big brother, from docent to
volunteering at an animal shelter, the best jobs you
can ever have pay absolutely nothing.

~

Some people hit the playground running.

Retirement is sad when your work is your life—
but a joy when your life is your work.

~

A good salesman is a chameleon with
rhinoceros hide and the persistence
of a mosquito in your bedroom at night.

~

A boring career finds its consolation
in extreme recreation.

~

Among the many advantages of being extremely
busy are having less work assigned to you,
seeming more important than you are,
and always having a ready excuse.

~

The perfect waiter is attentive, accommodating,
informative—and just a touch subservient.

Students will always love a teacher
who is in love with teaching.

～

The workaholic fears not
being missed when he's on vacation.

～

"I hear you" is a nice way of dodging the issue.

～

The longest question directed at a speaker
invariably contains no question at all.

～

Those who expect to live dull lives
after college tend to party hardest.

～

When the boss is nuts
the office becomes an asylum.

Talking often impersonates teaching.

～

Natural leaders are not created
in leadership training seminars.

～

Interesting work is a
bargain over boring work,
even at half the pay.

～

Many consultants are rarely consulted.

～

Productivity increases because ten percent of the
employees are willing to do the additional work
assigned to the other ninety percent.

～

Always respect that people who do menial work
must try to preserve their dignity in small ways.

I'm not lazy—I just like to work gently.

~

"I was multitasking"—that's what
type A personalities say when
they've messed up their work.

~

Better to have had a career as a good worker
than as a terrible boss.

~

Ambition is a race in which you
are permitted to make many false starts.

~

Most people will never know
anything better than a job.

~

When someone asks you what you do,
you could say, "Do about what?"

There are tasks we never get to because
they're too exhausting even to think about.

~

You can make your point without
throwing in the history of the world.

~

You imagined that a workaholic would be
productive, until you had one working for you.

~

Every interruption adds twice
its length to the task.

~

Necessity is also the mother of shoddy things
thrown together at the last minute.

~

I'd rather hire a carpenter who writes poetry
than a poet who does carpentry.

Employees are not slaves—because they
have the right to change masters.

∼

There's nothing wrong with
entering a career through a back door—
but you had better be a fast learner.

∼

There are jobs that are very stressful and
then there are the people
who find any job very stressful.

∼

There is as much dignity, and as much
humiliation, in cleaning the toilets in the
White House as there is in being president.

∼

For most people, the job is the life: a man does not
say that he is a father and a husband,
he says that he is a carpenter.

You knew the nail was bending,
so why did you keep hitting it?

~

There are a thousand ways to prostitute yourself,
sex being only one of them.

~

The boss may complain, but does he offer
to swap jobs with you?

~

The first lesson of serving the rich
is to become invisible.

~

A simple exchange of time for money—
it's called a job.

~

In exchanging time for money most people
discover that their time is worth very little.

If you are a lawyer, for God's sake don't talk like
one with your friends—there are no rules of
evidence in real life.

~

No one who serves is ever really grateful
for a gratuity.

~

A job is a collar that chafes.

~

Every job description contains a little humiliation.

~

There is no job description that contains
the word "security."

~

Once you discover that you are actually good at
something, you begin to think that you
might be good at other things.

I'm not afraid of hard work—being at home
with my family, now that's scary!

∾

To say something is "academic" reveals the
lack of respect you have for those who teach.

∾

Coffee brings the mind to work, and
alcohol enables the mind to leave it.

∾

No one knows more, and is paid less,
than a farmer.

∾

Do what needs to be done,
without talking it to death.

∾

On a planet on which a day is eighty-seven hours
long, I might manage to clear my desk.

Retirement is having three and a half
weekends a week.

≈

The first rule of operating heavy equipment
is to not kill the guy with the shovel.

≈

A lawyer pleads for the freedom of a man
he would hate to meet in a dark alley.

≈

A deadline alters time and space—one can
accomplish a month of work in the day before it.

≈

Compared to a farm or a factory,
an office is a very unproductive place.

≈

Comfortably wrapped in my white skin, I grumble
about preferences for people of other colors.

People who pretend to have a career
are actually rather common.

≈

A pedant has many ways to
amplify a small thought.

≈

A true perfectionist never finishes anything.

≈

Jobs have grown wings.

≈

We take for granted the competence
of the men who maintain elevators,
but not that of presidents and CEOs.

≈

If you would like to achieve an office
with a view at an early age, become a roofer.

Networking in a roomful of networkers
is like going fishing in a fish market.

~

We Americans are good at driving large trucks,
but we prefer to import our doctors and engineers.

~

A very easy job makes for a very long day at work.

~

Luckiest are those who always knew
what they wanted to do in life.

~

Sometimes you have to do the work
and hope the career materializes.

~

The best way to work with people who
get things done is to stay out of their way.

Difficult people enjoy meetings—
impossible people adore them.

∾

Don't do any work that you
wouldn't sign your name to.

∾

The "meeting face" is an alert mask concealing a
mind that is occupied with personal matters.

∾

There are few secrets of success, but plenty of
people making a good living selling them.

∾

We do ten things poorly,
when we should be doing one thing well.

∾

At peak performance there is nothing in the
universe, but the task at hand.

𝒞

Creating Epigrams

A ny articulate person is capable of creating an epigram because the raw material of an epigram is having lived while thinking. There is something thrilling about hearing yourself quoted. You have said something worth repeating. You are a sage! It is a little taste of immortality. You begin to dream of a spot in *Bartlett's Familiar Quotations.*

If you would like to try your hand, write out an observation or an opinion. Don't worry about how many words it takes to express the thought. Examine your idea. What is the essence of it? Begin to trim unnecessary clauses and words. Always keep in mind the immortal words of Strunk & White in *The Elements of Style*: "Omit unnecessary words".

If you get stuck, leave it and return later, always looking for the essence of your thought. The original thought may change; a new thought will emerge. You are trying for brevity—but if you have something worth saving, two or three lines are acceptable.

Try not to use long Latin words, adverbs, proper names, slang, topical references, qualifiers, foreign words or expressions, parenthetical statements, suppositions, or ephemeral expressions. Plain language will do. Think big. Don't try to be clever. You are looking for something timeless about the human condition.

About the Author

Michael Lipsey grew up surrounded by a large library of books and music in Chicago. He read the Great Books at Shimer College and remains an active observer of intellectual, religious, and popular culture. He has written many articles on management, employment, remodeling, music, dance, and community issues. When he isn't writing, he gardens, creates lacquered mirrors with quotations, and enjoys folk dancing; and gives thanks every day for the splendor of Marin County, California.